AF437627

Surah Al-Fatiha
As Explained By
Tafsir
Ibn Kathir
and
As-Sadi

Ibn Kathir
Abdur Rahman Nasir As-Sadi

01: The Tafsir of Surah Al-Fatiha (Opening of the Quran)

Which was revealed in Makkah

This Surah is named al-Fatihah (Opening) because it is the opening of the Qur'an. It is the first surah in accordance with the order of the Mushaf, as well as the first sura that a Muslim reads when performing prayers.

The names of Surah al-Fatihah

1. Ummul-Kitab (Mother of the Book)

The meaning of the book here is the Qur'an.

2. Ummul-Qur'an (Mother of the Qur'an)

These two names are based on the hadith narrated by Abu Hurairah, the Messenger of Allah (peace and blessings of Allaah be upon him) said,

الْحَمْدُ لِلَّهِ رَبِّ الْعَالَمِينَ أُمُّ الْقُرْآنِ وَأُمُّ الْكِتَابِ وَالسَّبْعُ الْمَثَانِي وَالْقُرْآنُ الْعَظِيمُ

"Praise be to God, Lord of the Worlds. It is the mother of the Qur'an, the mother of the Book, the Seven Oft- Recited (verses), and the Great Qur'an." (At-Tirmidhi, 3123; Abu Dawud, 1457 with authentic status. There are also other lines narrated by Bukhari, 4704; Ahmad, 2/448)

3. Al-Hamd (Praise)

As explained in the hadith above, Alhamdulillahi Rabbil 'Alamin is Ummul Qur'an....

4. As-Salah (Salat)

It is called so because Abu Hurairah narrated that the Messenger of Allah (peace and blessings of Allah be upon him) said in the Qudsi hadith, Allah said,

قَسَمْتُ الصَّلَاةَ بَيْنِي وَبَيْنَ عَبْدِي نِصْفَيْنِ،

"I divided the prayer between Me and My servant into two halves…"

5. Ash-Shifa (Cure/Healer)

It is called that based on the hadith narrated by Abu Sa'id al-Khudri. The Prophet (peace and blessings of Allah be upon him) said,

"Fatihatul-Kitab (Surah al-Fatihah) is Shifa (cure) for all diseases."

6. Ar-Ruqyah

It is called that based on the hadith of Abû Sa'id al-Khudri when he recited it to treat a man who was stung by a venomous animal. After that, Rasulullah (peace and blessings of Allah be upon him) said to Abu Sa'id al-Khudri:

وَمَا يُدْرِيكَ أَنَّهَا رُقْيَةٌ

How did you know that Surah al- Fatihah is a ruqyah (spell).

7. Asâsul-Qur'ân (Foundation of the Quran)

This is based on the expression of Ibn Abbas who said, "The principle of al-Fâtihah is al-Basmalah."

8. Al-Waqiyah (Preventer)

This is based on the opinion of Sufyan bin Uyainah who called al-Fatihah as al-Waqiyah, because Surah al-Fatihah can protect a believer who reads it.

9. Al-Kafiyah (Enough)

This is based on the opinion of Yahya bin Abi Kathir, who according to him al-Fatihah is sufficient even without the other surahs, but the other surahs cannot be sufficient without the surah al-Fatihah.

10. Al-Kanz (Content)

It is called that because the content of meaning in surah al-Fâtihah contains the main messages from the contents of the Qur'an.

Makkiyyah, Totaling 7 Verses

Scholars differ on whether al-Fatihah is included in the Makkiyyah (revealed before the Hijrah) or Madaniyyah (revealed after the Hijrah). According to Ibn Abbas, Qatâdah, and Abû al-'Aliyah, Surah al- Fatihah is Makkiyyah. As for Abu Hurairah, Mujâ-hid, and 'Atha' bin Yasar say that this is a Madaniyyah surah.

Another opinion is that al-Fâtihah was sent down twice, first in Mecca, second in Medina. Some scholars are of the opinion that half of it descended in Mecca, while the other half in Medina. However, this opinion is very odd.

The strongest opinion is the first opinion, namely Makkiyyah. The basis is the word of God,

وَلَقَدْ ءَاتَيْنَٰكَ سَبْعًا مِّنَ الْمَثَانِي

And verily We have given you as-sab'ul matsâni (seven verses that are read repeatedly, that is Surah Al-Fatiha)... (al-Hijr [15]:87)

This Surah al-Hijr is included in Makkiyyah. What is meant by as-sab`ul matsânî (seven verses that are read repeatedly) is surah al-Fatihah. Sab'un (seven) because the verses number seven. It is called matsânî (repetitive) because it is recited often (in the prayer). It is read in every rakaat of prayer.

Thus, based on the argument above, the number of verses in surah al-Fâtihah is seven. There is a need to ignore opinions that say the number of verses is six or eight, because this contradicts the above verse and the opinion of the majority of scholars.

Scholars differ in calculating the seven verses of surah al-Fatihah because of the status of "Basmallah". We'll talk about that in a bit, in sha'Allah (If Allah wills).

According to the scholars, the number of words in al-Fatihah is 25 words, while the letters are 113 letters.

Why is it called Ummul-Kitab?

Surah al-Fatihah is called Ummul-Kitab because it is the first surah written in the Qur'an. Also it comes in the beginning of reading in prayer. This is Imam Bukhari's opinion.

Other scholars say, this surah is called Ummul-Kitâb because all the meanings contained in the Qur'an refer to what is contained in it.

Please see what is explained by Ibn Jarir ath-Thabârî below:

The Arabs name each set or the leading part of a thing if it has a continuation that follows it (like the imam in a large mosque) with the term umm (mother, parent). For that, they named the skin covering the brain with the term ummur-ra'si (mother of the head). They also named the banner or flag under which the team gathered with the term ummul-jaisy (mother of the team). Because of this, Makkah was named Ummul-Qurâ. Because, it is a city that gathers all the countries around it. There is also an opinion that says Ummul-Qurâ (mother of the country) because the earth is rounded starting from it.

Al-Fâtihah is the first complete surah revealed. As for what was revealed before, it is the beginning of surah al-Muddassir, al-Muzzammil, al-'Alaq, and al-Qalam. As for the verse of the Qur'an that was revealed for the first time, it is the beginning of surah al-'Alaq.

Hadith about the Priority of al-Fâtihah

1. Hadith narrated by Abu Sa'id bin Al-Mu'alla (Allah be pleased with him):

I was praying. The Messenger of Allah called me but I did not answer him until I finished praying. Then, I came to him, and he said: Why didn't you come to me immediately?

I replied, "O Messenger of Allah, I was praying."

He (peace and blessings of Allah be upon him) said: Didn't God say, O you who believe, fulfill the call of God and the call of the Messenger when your Messenger calls you to something that gives you life. (al-Anfal [8]: 24)

He (peace and blessings of Allah be upon him) said again: Verily, I will teach you the greatest surah in the Qur'an before you leave this mosque.

Then, he held my hand.

When he was about to leave the mosque, I asked, "O Messenger of Allah, you have said that you will teach me one of the greatest surahs of the Qur'an."

He replied: Yes, Al-Handu lillahi rabbil 'alamin. It is the seven repeated verses and al-'azhim (Glorious) al-Qur'an that was given to me.

Bukhari, 4474, 4647, 4703, 5006; Abd Dawud, 1458; an-Nasat, 913 (2/139); Ibnu Majah, 3758; Ahmad, 3/ 450, ad-Darimi, 2/ 445; Abu Ya'la, 6837

2. Hadith from Abu Hurairah (Allah be pleased with him):

The Prophet (peace and blessings of Allah be upon him) once went out to meet Ubay bin Ka'ab (Allah be pleased with him) who was praying. He called, O Ubay!

Ubay turned his head but did not answer. Then he called again, O Ubay!

Ubay hastened his prayer.

After Ubay finished the prayer, he met the Messenger of Allah (peace and blessings of Allah be upon him), then greeted him, "Assalamu'alaika ya Rasulullah!"

Rasulullah replied, Wa 'alaika salam! O Ubay, what prevented you from answering me when I called you?
He said: "O Messenger of Allah, verily I was praying."

The Messenger of God (peace and blessings of Allah be upon him) said: Did you not find what God revealed to me that fulfill the call of God and the call of the Messenger when the Messenger calls you to something that gives you life?

"O Messenger of Allah, I promise not to repeat it again."

The Messenger of Allah said: Would you like it if I taught you a surah that has never been revealed in the Torah, the Injil, the Psalms, and there is no similar surah in the Qur'an?

He replied, "Yes, O Messenger of Allah."

The Prophet said, "In fact, I really hope that before I leave the door of this mosque you will know about it."

Then, Rasulullah held my hand while talking to me. I slowed my pace for fear that he would reach the door of the mosque before he finished hi conversation.

When we approached the door, I asked, "O Messenger of Allah, what surah did you promise to teach me?"

He said: What do you read when you open your prayer?

Then I recited surah Ummul-Qur'ân (al-Fâtihah) to him.

After that, he said, "By Allah in whose hand my soul is, Allah has never revealed in the Tawrah, the Injil, the Zabur or the Furqan a Surah like it. It is the seven repeated verses that I was given."

At-Tirmidhi in Fadháil-Qur'an, 2875; an-Nasa1, 914; Ahmad, 2/412-413; ad-Darimi, 2/446; Abu Ya'la, 6482; Hakim, 1/557, authenticated by adz-Dzahabi

3. Hadith from Abdullah bin Jâbir (Allah be pleased with him) which tells the following:

I came to the Messenger of Allah who at that time he had poured water for ablution, so I said, "Assalamu'alaika, O Messenger of Allah!" However, he did not answer me. I said again, "Assalamu `alaika, O Messenger of Allah!" However, he still did not answer me. Then I said again, "Assalamu 'alaika, O Messenger of Allah!" However, he still did not answer me.

The Prophet then walked and I was behind him until he entered his tent. Then, I entered the mosque, then sat in a sad state.

The Messenger of God came out to meet me in a state of purification, then said, Wa `alaika salam wa rahmatullah wa barakatuh, wa `alaika salam wa rahmatullah wa barakatuh, wa 'alaika salam wa rahmatullah wa barakatuh!

Then, he (peace and blessings of Allah be upon him) said: Shall I teach you, O 'Abdullah bin Jabir, one of the best surahs in the Qur'an?

I replied, "Yes, O Messenger of Allah!"

The Messenger of Allah said: Read alhamdulillahi rabbil àlamin (al-Fatihah) until it is finished.

Of the three hadiths narrated above-as well as similar hadiths-some scholars make the argument that it is permissible to prioritize one surah over another. Among the scholars who hold this opinion are Ishaq bin Rahawaih, Abu Bakr bin al-'Arabî, and Ibn al-Haffär from the Maliki School.

There are also a number of scholars such as al-Asy'ari, Abû Bakar al-Bâqilanî, and Abû Hâtim al-Busti who are of the opinion that it is not permissible to prioritize a surah because all of them are Kalámullâh (words of Allah). The goal is not to think that prioritizing something means there is a lack of something that is outweighed by its primacy. All surahs in the Qur'an are main, have the same level of primacy, because all of them are Kalâmullâh.

4. Hadith from Abû Sa'id al-Khudri (Allah be pleased with him), he narrates that when he was on a journey, suddenly a young slave girl came. Then she said, "Surely the leader of the tribe is stung by a poisoned animal, while our people are away. Is there anyone among you who can do ruqyah (healing with spells)?"

One of us stood up, even though we had never noticed before that he could perform ruqyah. Later, the man performed ruqyah and it turned out that the leader of the tribe was cured. So, the leader of the tribe ordered to pay us thirty goats and give us a drink of milk. When the man returned, we asked him, "Are you able to perform ruqyah or are you good at performing ruqyah?"

He replied, "No, I only perform ruqyah by reading Ummul-Kitâb. (al-Fâti- hah)."

We said, "Don't talk about anything before we arrive and ask the Messenger of Allah."

When we arrived in Madinah, we told the Messenger of Allah about it and he replied: How did you know that al-Fâtihah is ruqyah? Share it and give me a portion of it.

According to some narrations, it was Abu Sa'id al-Khudri who performed ruqyah on the person who was stung.

5. Hadith from Abdullah bin 'Abbas, he narrates:

When we were with the Prophet who was with the Angel Gabriel (Jibreel), suddenly the Prophet heard a noise above him. Gabriel then raised his eyes to the sky and said, "This is a sign that the doors of heaven are being opened, which have never been opened before."
Then, an angel came down and said to the Messenger of Allah, "Rejoice with the two lights that have been given to you. No prophet before you was ever given both, namely Fâtihatul- Kitab and the last verses of Surah Al- Baqarah. You will not read a letter of them, but will gain its benefit."

6. Hadith of Abu Hurairah (Allah be pleased with him) that the Messenger of Allah (peace and blessings of Allah be upon him) said:

Whoever prays without reading Ummul- Kitab (al-Fatihah), then his prayer is not perfect, then his prayer is not perfect, then his prayer is not perfect.

Then, it was said to Abu Hurairah, "Verily, we pray behind the imam."

Abu Hurairah replied, "Read it for yourself because I have heard the Messenger of Allah say:

Allah said, "I have divided the prayer between Me and My servant into two parts and for My servant what he asks for." When he said, "All praise be to God, the Lord of the worlds," God said, "My servant has praised Me." When he said, "The Most Gracious and Most Merciful," God said, "My servant has glorified Me." When he said, "He who controls the Day of Retribution," then God said, "My servant has glorified Me," or, "My servant has surrendered to Me." When he said, "Only You do we worship and only You do we ask for help," then God said, "This is between Me and My servants and for My servants is what is asked." When he said, "Show us the straight path, which is the path of those who You have bestowed favors on them, it is not their way that You are angry with and it is not their way that goes astray", then God said, "This is for My servant and for My servant is what he asked for."

The Importance of Reading al-Fatihah in Prayer

From the authentic hadith above, several conclusions can be drawn related to surah al-Fatihah.

The word "prayer" in the hadith "Qasamtu ash-salâh baini wa baina abdi" is reading surah al-Fatihah. So, the meaning of the hadith is: "I divide the recitation of al-Fatihah in prayer between me and my servant into two parts…"

The word "prayer" in the Qur'an is sometimes intended as a reading in prayer.

This is as stated in His word:

Do not raise your voice in your prayer and do not lower it and find a middle way between the two. (al-Isra' [17]: 110)

The word "prayer" is sometimes used with the meaning of reciting al-Fâtihah in prayer. This shows how important and great the recitation of al-Fatiha is in prayer. This is the most sublime pillar of prayer.

The mention of the term "prayer" when the meaning is "al-Fatihah reading" illustrates the importance of this section. All of this shows that in prayer, it is obligatory to read the Qur'an.

The Obligation to Read al-Fatihah in Every Rak'at

The hadith above shows the importance of reading al-Fatihah in prayer. The question arises, is the recitation of al- Fatihah a pillar of prayer? If you don't read it, your prayer becomes invalid?

There are two opinions about this:

1. According to Abu Hanifah and his followers, reading al-Fatihah is not a must in prayer. What is obligatory is to read whatever is in the Qur'an, either al-Fàti- hah or other surahs. This is based on the word of God:

Therefore read what is easy (for you) of the Quran... (al-Muzzammil [73]: 20)

In addition, the evidence of the generality of the hadith narrated from Abu Hurairah about the narration of a person who made a mistake in his prayer. The Prophet (peace and blessings of Allah be upon him) said,

"When you are about to perform your prayer, say takbir and then read what is easy for you from the Qur'an."

The Messenger of Allah (peace and blessings of Allah be upon him) ordered the man to read what was easy from the Qur'an. He did not determine that as al-Fatihah.

2. The opinion of the three imams: Imam Malik, Shafi'i, and Ahmad bin Hanbal and the majority of the scholars. They emphasized that reading surah al-Fatihah in prayer is obligatory. In other words, prayer is not valid if you do not read surah al-Fatihah.

This is based on hadith:

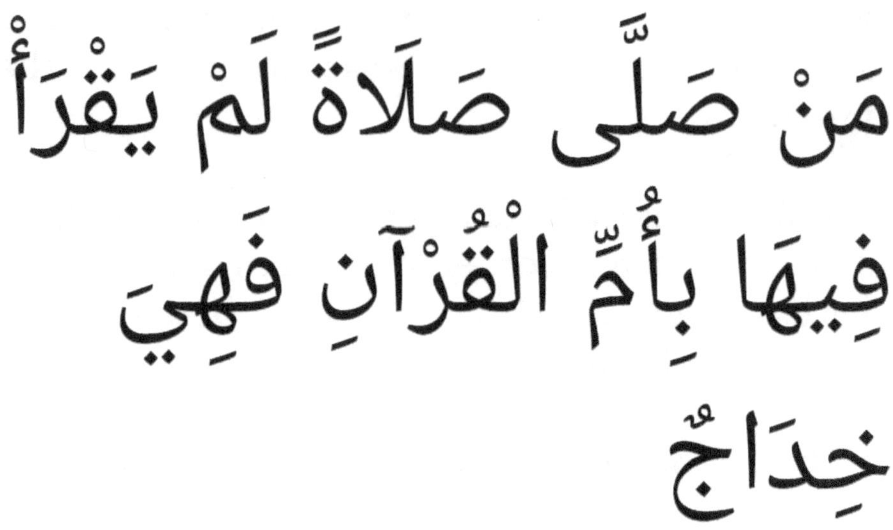

Whoever prays and does not read sura al- Fatihah, then his prayer is khadaj (imperfect).

What is meant by khadaj is less. The word khadaj in this hadith can be interpreted as "imperfect".

Another argument is the hadith narrated by Abu Ubadah bin Shamit, the Messenger of Allah said,

"There is no prayer for one who does not recite the Opening of the Book."

People who do not read Fâtihatul-Kitab are not considered to have prayed.

3. Some scholars are of the opinion that reading surah al-Fâtihah does not have to be read for every unit (rakah), but only for most of the units.

4. The majority of scholars are of the opinion that reading al-Fatihah is obligatory for every unit of prayer. This applies to obligatory prayers or sunnah prayers.

The strongest opinion is that reciting al-Fatihah in every rak'ah of prayer is obligatory. In any prayer, both obligatory and sunnah. Al-Fatihah is the pillar of prayer. If it is not read, it cancels the rakat of the prayer.

Tafsir Isti'adhah (seeking refuge)

Istiadhah (or ta'awwudz) is saying a'ûdzubillahi minas-shaithânir rajîm (I seek refuge in Allah to be protected from Satan's interference).

The Need to be Protected from Satan's Influence

Allah commands us to seek protection from satan when reading the Qur'an. Likewise when doing other worship activities. Especially when disturbed by evil thoughts.

Be forgiving and tell people to do what is good, and turn away from foolish people. And if you are tempted by the devil (if an evil whisper comes to you from Satan), then seek refuge in Allah. (al-A'râf [7]: 199-200)

Reject their bad deeds with better ones. We know better what they describe. And say, "My Lord, I seek refuge in You from the whispers of Satan. And I seek refuge in You, my Lord, from their coming to me." (al- Mu'minûn [23]: 96-98)

And good and evil are not the same. Reject (the evil) in a better way. So, suddenly the person with whom there is enmity between you and him seems to have become a very loyal friend. Those good qualities are not awarded except to those who are patient and are not awarded except to those who have the great portion (of happiness in the Hereafter). And if the devil bothers you with something, ask God for protection. Indeed, He is the All-Hearing and All- Knowing. (Fussilat [41]: 34-36)

Through the verses above, Allah commands us to be lenient with enemies from among humans, to do good to him so that he is aware and returns to his original good character, namely returning to friendship. Meanwhile, to Satan, the greatest human enemy, Allah commands us to take refuge in Him. There is no good from diplomacy with satan (being lenient to him) and doing good to him. He always spoiled Adam's children and grandchildren. This was the fruit of his deep enmity with Adam and his descendants.

Satan's Hostility to Humans

Among the verses that explain Satan's hostility to humans:

O son of Adam, don't you ever be deceived by the devil as he took your parents out of heaven, he took off their clothes to show them their aurat. Indeed, he and his followers see you from a place where you cannot see them. Verily, We have made the devils the leaders of the disbelievers. (al-A'râf [7]: 27)

Indeed, satan is an enemy to you, so consider him (your) enemy, because actually he only invites his group (followers) so that they become residents of the burning hell. (Fâthir [35]: 6)

Will you take him and his descendants as leaders rather than Me, while they are your enemies? It is very bad that the devil is a substitute for the unjust people. (al-Kahf [18]: 50)

Satan's promise to God

Satan replied,

"By your might, I will mislead them all, except Your servants who are sincere (chosen) among them." (Shád [38]: 82-83)

This sworn enemy, the devil, has promised to lead Adam's descendants astray. He also swore to God about it.

God said:

When you recite the Qur'an, ask Allah for protection from the cursed devil. Indeed, the devil has no power over those who believe and trust in their Lord. In fact, his (satan's) power is only over those who take him as a leader and over those who associate him with God. (an-Nahl [16]: 98-100)

Allah commands us through this last verse to seek refuge from the devil when we want to read the Qur'an.

Seeking refuge before reciting the Qur'an

Scholars differ on when to read ta'awwudz: Before or after reading the Quran?

1. Ibnu Sirin, Ibrâhîm an-Nakha'i, and Dâwûd bin 'Ali azh-Zhâhiri, who attributed the opinion of Imam Mâlik bin Anas to the opinion that reading ta'awwudz is done after reading the Qur'an. This refers to the apparent verse to reject the feeling of ujub (self-pride) after doing worship. This is a strange opinion.

2. Ta'awwudz is done before and after reading the Qur'an. This brings the two together that is the opinion which says at the beginning and the other opinion which says at the end. This is also attributed as Imam Malik's opinion. However, even this opinion is odd.

3. Ta'awwudz is done before reciting the Qur'an to reject the devil's interference. This opinion is the strongest.

$$\text{فَإِذَا قَرَأْتَ الْقُرْآنَ فَاسْتَعِذْ}$$

$$\text{بِاللَّهِ مِنَ الشَّيْطَانِ الرَّجِيمِ}$$

So when you [want to] recite the Qur'an, seek refuge with Allah from Shaytan, the outcast (the cursed one).

This verse has the meaning that if you want to read the Qur'an, ask Allah for protection from the accursed devil. This verse is similar in meaning to the practice of ablution before praying.

Allah said,

O you who believe, when you want to pray, wash your face and your hands up to the elbows, and wipe your head and (wash) your feet up to the ankles. (al- Mâ'idah [5]: 6)

The meaning of the verse above is, if you want to pray, wash your face and hands. It is common knowledge that ablution is performed before prayer, not during or after prayer. Similarly, the recitation of ta'awwudz is done before reciting the Qur'an.

Prophet's guidance

The arguments that strengthen the above opinion are all valid. Among them:

1. Hadith from Sulaiman bin Shurad, who said, "There were two men who insulted each other by the side of the Messenger of Allah (peace and blessings of Allah be upon him), while we were by his side. One of them insulted the other in a state of anger. Then, the Prophet said:

"Really, I know very well that there is one sentence that if he said will remove his anger, that is the sentence, A'ûdzu billâhi minash-shaithânir-rajim (I seek refuge with Allah from the cursed Satan)."

Then, we said to the angry one, "Didn't you hear what the Messenger of God said earlier?" The angry man said, "I am not a madman." He refused to read it.

2. Abu Sa'id al-Khudri said, "When the Messenger of Allah wanted to perform the Night Prayer, he

began by reciting the Takbeer (saying "Allahu Akbar"; Allah is Greater) and then reciting,

سُبْحَانَكَ اللّٰهُمَّ وَبِحَمْدِكَ، وَتَبَارَكَ اسْمُكَ، وَتَعَالَى جَدُّكَ، وَلَا إِلَهَ غَيْرُكَ

"All praise is due to You, O God, for Your glory, for the sanctity of Your name, and high is Your majesty, there is no God that has the right to be worshiped but You."

Then he (peace and blessings of Allah be upon him) read, "there is no God worthy of worship except Allah" - three times.

He (peace and blessings of Allah be upon him) would then read,

أَعُوذُ بِاللهِ السَّمِيعِ الْعَلِيمِ مِنَ الشَّيْطَانِ الرَّجِيمِ مِنْ هَمْزِهِ وَنَفْخِهِ وَنَفْثِهِ

I seek refuge in Allah, the All-Hearing and All-Knowing, from the temptation of the accursed devil, that is, from the narrowness, the blowing, and the blowing of his seductions (which lures to arrogance and poems)."

In addition to the above hadith, there are several similar hadiths. For example hadith from Ibn Mas'ud and Abu Umamah al-Bahili.

In conclusion, reading ta'awwudz is done before you are going to read the Qur'an.

Ta'awwudz is the Recommended Sunnah

The basic question is, is reading ta'awwudz obligatory or just a suggestion? The scholars differed.

The reading of ta'awwudz is obligatory, both in prayer and outside of prayer. This opinion was put forward by 'Atha' bin Abi Rabbah with reference to the clear verse,

When you read the Qur'an, you should ask Allah for protection.
(an-Nahl [16]: 98)

The order in the verse shows that it is obligatory to read to ta'awwudz. The Prophet (peace and blessings of Allah be upon him) used to read it.

Apart from that, what is more important is the reason to prevent the devil's interference from coming. This is mandatory. Rule of fiqh: "If an obligation cannot be perfect except with something else, then that something also becomes obligatory". So, reading ta'awwudz becomes obligatory because it will prevent satanic disturbance from coming.

Reading ta'awwudz is a sunnah that is recommended to be read, both in the obligatory prayer, the sunnah prayer, and before reciting the Qur'an. This is the strongest opinion.

Benefits of Ta'awudz

Among the benefits of ta'awwudz:

1. Purification of the mouth. In general, with the mouth a person says useless things, dirty words, swearing, and even lies.

2. Ta'awwudz perfumes the mouth and implies readiness to recite the Kalâmullah (Al-Qur'an).

3. Reading ta'awwudz means asking Allah for help, acknowledging His power and strength, and acknowledging that the reader is a weak servant (of Allah) and does not have any power.

Among the weaknesses of a servant is not being able to fight the devil's interference. Therefore, a servant must ask for protection from God Almighty and the help of God to reject the disturbance.

There are two enemies for a Muslim: the hidden enemy, namely Satan, and the real enemy, namely the disbelievers.

Whoever is killed by an open enemy (unbeliever), then he is martyred. However, if a person dies because of the temptation of a hidden enemy (the devil), he dies in a state of misery.

Satan can see humans, but humans cannot see him. Therefore, a believer must seek protection from Allah who sees Satan, while Satan cannot see Him.

The definition of Isti'adhah itself means: Asking Allah for protection, relying completely on Allah for protection from all evil and seeking refuge with Him from the evil of every evil creature.

The meaning of "I take refuge with Allah from the temptation of the cursed devil" is to seek refuge in God from the cursed devil. I ask God to protect me from the devil who can cause harm to my religion and my world, or I ask God that the devil should not prevent me from doing what I am commanded to do, or that the devil cannot push me to do things which are prohibited.

No one can prevent satan's harassment of believers except Allah Himself.

Origin of the word 'Shaytan'

There are two opinions of scholars about the origin of the word satan in Arabic:

1. The word shaytan is taken from a word that means "far". This is understandable because demons are fundamentally far different from human nature. Also shaytan is far away because of his iniquity and defiance of all goodness. That is why, Satan can be sure to be far from God's mercy.

2. Some scholars argue that the word shaytan is taken from a word which means "burning hot".

This is understandable because Satan was created from fire and will be tormented in the afterlife by fire
also.

Of the two opinions, the strongest is the first opinion.

Satan is always an infidel, both the Shayatin (devils) among Jinn and Humans.

The word Su is used to denote the disobedient attitude of the jinn, human, and animal types.

Jinns who disbelieve are shaytan, so do human beings who disbelieve are shaytan.

And thus We made enemies for every prophet, namely the devils (of the type of) humans and (type of) jinn, some of them whispered to some of the others. (al-An'am [6]: 112)

Abû Dzarr al-Ghifârî narrates that the Messenger of Allah (peace and blessings of Allah be upon him) said, "The ones who can interrupt the prayer are women, donkeys, and black dogs." I asked, "What's the difference between a black, red, and yellow dog?" He replied, "The black dog is a devil."

The Commander of the Faithful, 'Umar bin al-Khaththâb, once rode a Berthawn (huge camel). The animal walked arrogantly. The more he was beaten to make him run fast, the more arrogant he became.

'Umar (Allah be pleased with him) dismounted the animal and said, "You do not provide a vehicle for me except on this satanic vehicle! I did not get off it until I had felt something strange in my heart."

"The Cursed and Exiled": The meaning of Ar-Rajim

الرحيم in the utterance of مِنَ الشَّيْطَانِ الرَّحِيمِ

The word is patterned as ism fa'il (doer), but means mafûl (object). The word means shaytaan who are expelled and away from all goodness.

The use of the word (root word with the meaning of throwing or expelling) is contained in the word of God:

Verily, We adorned the heavens which are close to the stars and We made them as missiles to drive away the Shayatin. (al- Mulk [67]: 5)

Verily, We have adorned the closest sky with ornaments, namely the stars and have protected it from every satan who is very rebellious. The satan could not hear the angels talking and they were pelted from all around to drive them away, and for them is eternal torment. However, whoever among them steals the conversation, he will be chased by a flaming torch. (ash-Sâffât [37]: 6-10)

The verses above inform us that Allah ordered the angels to stone satans when they tried to ascend to heaven. They were pelted with stars and were chased away from the sky.

Verse 1

(1) In the name of Allah, the Most Gracious, the Most Merciful!

This means: I start in the name of Allah. From the lexical analysis of this phrase, it is clear that all the beautiful names of the Supreme Lord are meant.

Allah is one of these names, meaning 'God, who is deified and worshipped; The only one who deserves to be worshiped by virtue of His divine qualities - the qualities of perfection and impeccability'.

The beautiful names Gracious and Merciful testify to His great mercy, embracing everything and every creature. The mercy of Allah will be fully awarded to His God-fearing servants who follow the path of God's prophets and messengers. And all other creatures will receive only a part of God's grace.

You should know that all righteous scholars unanimously spoke about the need for faith in Allah and His divine qualities (attributes). The Lord is Gracious and Merciful, that is, He possesses mercy, which is manifested on His servants. All blessings and bounties are one of the many manifestations of His mercy and compassion. The same can be said about other names of Allah. He is "All-Knowing", that is, He has knowledge of everything that exists. He is "All-Powerful", that is, He has power and might over all creatures.

The companions began the recitation of the Qur'an with the basmalah (Bismillaahir Rahmaanir Raheem).

Scholars have agreed that basmalah is part of one verse from surah an-Naml (chapter 27).

God said:

Indeed, it is from Sulaiman and its content is: In the name of Allah, the Most Gracious, the Most Merciful. That you should not be arrogant towards me and come to me as people who surrender. (an-Naml [27]: 30-31)

Basmalah, Part of al-Fatihah and All Surahs

Scholars differ on the position of basmalah in the Qur'an. Among these opinions:

1. Basmalah is a separate verse at the beginning of each surah, except for surah at- Taubah.

This is the opinion of the companions (Allah be pleased with them), such as Ibn Abbas, Ibn 'Umar, Ibn Zubair, Ali bin Abi Talib, and Abu Hurairah.

Besides them, this conclusion also refers to the opinion of tabi'in such as Atha, Thawus, Sa'id bin Zubair, Makhul, and az-Zuhri. This opinion is also held by 'Abdullah bin Mubarak, ash-Shafi'i, Ahmad bin Hanbal, Ishaq bin Rahawaih, and Abû 'Ubaid al- Qasim bin Salam.

2. Basmalah is not part of surah al- Fatihah, nor is it part of any other surah. This opinion is held by Imam Malik, Imam Abu Hanifah, and his followers.

3. Basmalah is part of surah al-Fâtihah, but not for other surahs. This opinion is based on Imam ash-Shafi'i.

4. Basmalah is a separate verse at the beginning of each surah. This opinion was presented by Dawud azh-Zhàhiri and Ahmad bin Hambal in a narration.

5. Basmalah is part of the verse from the beginning of each surah in the Qur'an. This opinion also relied on Imam ash-Shafi'i.

Of all the existing opinions about the basmalah position, the strongest opinion is the first. Basmalah is part of surah al-Fâtihah and other surahs, except for surah at-Taubah.

Recitation of Basmalah in Salat (the prayer)

Scholars have different opinions about reciting basmalah in prayer and saying it aloud in prayer. There are three opinions on this matter:

1. Basmalah is read at the beginning of each surah and is read in each rak'ah of prayer and must be read aloud in loud prayers. This is Imam Shafi'i's opinion with the following argument:

Basmalah is part of surah al-Fâtihah, so the law is the same as the law for reading al-Fatihah. When the recites al-Fâtihah, it is obligatory to recite the basmalah as well.

• Abu Hurairah (Allah be pleased with him) prayed and recited basmalah in his recitation. As soon as he finished the prayer, he said to the person behind him, "Indeed, I am the person whose prayer is most similar to the prayer of the Messenger of Allah."

Anas bin Mâlik was asked about the Prophet's recitation. Anas said, "The Prophet always lengthened his recitation." Then he recited bismillahir-rahmânir-rahim. He lengthens the recitation of bismillah, lengthens the recitation of rahmân, and also lengthens the recitation of raheem.

Umm Salamah (Allah be pleased with her) said that the Prophet (peace and blessings of Allah be upon him) read in an orderly manner the sentences bismillahir-rahmanirrahim, alhamdulillahi rabbil 'alamin, ar-rahmânir-rahim, maliki yaumid-din."

Anas bin Malik (Allah be pleased with him) narrates that Mu'awiyah bin Abi Sufyan (Allah be pleased with him) once prayed in Madinah and did not recite the Basmallah. Pilgrims from among the Muhajirin also protested. When Mu'awiyah prayed for the second time, he recited the Basmallah.

• A group of companions, tabi'in, the salaf and later scholars, recited the basmalah.

Among the companions (among the salaf): Abu Hurairah, Ibn Umar, Ibn Abbas, Mu'awiyah, and the four caliphs (Allah be pleased with them).

Among the tabi'in: Said bin Jubair, 'Ikrimah, Abû Qalabah, Zuhri, Ali bin Hasan, Muhammad bin Ali, Sa'id bin Mûsâyab, 'Atha', Thawus, Mujahid, Salim, Muhammad bin Ka' ab al-Qurdhi, Ubaid, Abu Bakar bin Muhammad bin Amr bin Hazm, Muhammad bin Munkadir, 'Ali bin Abdillah, Ibnu Abbas, Muhammad, Nafi' (maula Ibnu Umar), Zaid bin Aslam bin Abdul Aziz, and others.

2. Basmalah is recited in prayer, but should not be recited aloud in the prayer. This is the opinion of Abu Hanifah, Ahmad bin Hanbal, and Sufyân at-Thawri.

3. Basmalah cannot be recited at all, either in jahar (loud) prayers or in sirr (silent)prayers. This

opinion is held by Anas bin Malik. The arguments for the second and third groups are as follows:
Hadith from Aishah (Allah be pleased with her) that when the Prophet (peace and blessings of Allah be upon him) prayed he said takbir and then recited alhamdu lillâhi rabbil 'alamin.

Hadith from Anas bin Malik who once spoke to the Prophet, Abu Bakar, 'Umar, Uthmân, and they started their prayers by reading alhamdu lillâhi rabbil 'alamin.

In another narration from Anas, Rasulullah and his companions started the prayer by reading alhamdu lillâhi rabbil 'alamin and did not read bismillahirrahmanirrahim at the beginning or the end of the recitation.

A group of salaf and khalaf scholars, especially the Khulafaur-Rashidin, did not emphasize reciting the basmalah in prayer. What is certain, based on their history, basmalah is not invoked in the prayer. The scholars agree that the prayer of the person who recites the basmalah aloud is valid and so does the person who does not recite it aloud.

The strongest opinion is the first, which is to read the basmalah in the jahar (loud) prayer and to read the basmalah in every unit (of prayer), because the basmalah is part of surah al-Fâtihah.

Some of the Laws Related to Basmalah

Among the laws related to basmalah are as follows:

1. If a believer is overcome by anxiety, he should read ta`awwudz. If evil is overwritten, you should read basmalah so that you insult Satan.

Usamah bin 'Amir narrated, "I was once with the Messenger of Allah, suddenly his camel tripped, I spontaneously said, "Woe to (cursed) Satan!"

The Prophet (peace and blessings of Allah be upon him) said: Do not say, "Woe to Satan." If you say, "Woe to Satan," the devil gets bigger and says, "I defeated him with my power (with my strength I made him fall)." However, say, Bismillâh (in the name of Allah). If you say that, Satan will surely shrink until he becomes as small as a fly."

2. Reading basmalah will save the reader from the torment of hell fire.

Ibn Mas`ud narrates, "Whoever wants to be saved by Allah from the Zabaniyah (the tormentors of the sinners in hell) angels, then read 'bismillâhirrahmânirrahîm', Allah made each letter basmalah a stronghold and protector of every Zabaniyah angel."

3. It is sunnah to read basmalah for scholars when they are about to start their sermon.

4. It is sunnah to read basmalah when going to the restroom.

5. It is sunnah to read basmalah when doing ablution.

6. It is sunnah to read basmalah when you are starting to do dhikr to Allah.

7. It is sunnah to recite basmalah when slaughtering animals according to the Ash-Shafi'iyah school, and it is obligatory to say basmalah in other schools of thought.

8. It is sunnah to recite basmalah before having intercourse. The Messenger of Allah (peace and blessings of Allah be upon him) said: If you want to have a husband and wife relationship say, "In the name of Allah. O Allah, keep us away from the devil, and keep the devil away from what You bestowed on us." If it is destined for both of them to have children, Satan will not be able to harm the child."

9. It is sunnah to read basmalah when going to eat. The Messenger of Allah said to his stepson from Umm Salamah, `Umar bin Abi Salamah, "Say, 'Bismillah', eat with your right hand, and eat food that is close to you."

The Meaning of 'Allah'

Allah is the Special Name for the Lord of the Universe. This name is not used for anyone else. This blessed name refers to a number of the perfect attributes of Allah. Likewise His other names, are considered to be the attributes of this name. It is the Greatest Name of Allah.

Allah said:

He is Allaah, beside Whom La ilaha illa Huwa (none has the right to be worshipped but He) the Knower of the unseen and the seen. He is the Most Gracious, the Most Merciful. He is Allah, beside Whom La ilaha illa Huwa (none has the right to be worshipped but He), the King, the Holy, the One free from all defects, the Giver of security, the Watcher over His creatures, the Almighty, the Compeller, the Supreme. Glory be to Allah! (High is He) above all that they associate as partners with Him. He is Allaah, the Creator, the Inventor of all things, the Bestower of forms. To Him belong the Best Names. All that is in the heavens and the earth glorify Him. And He is the Almighty, the Wise) (59:22-24).

And (all) the Most Beautiful Names belong to Allaah, so call on Him by them. (7:180)

Say (O Muhammad) "Invoke Allaah or invoke the Most Gracious (Allah), by whatever name you invoke Him (it is the same), for to Him belong the Best Names.". (17:110)

The Prophet (peace and blessings of Allah be upon him) said, "Allaah has ninety-nine Names, one hundred minus one, whoever counts (and preserves) them, will enter Paradise."

The Meaning of Ar-Rahman Ar-Rahim - the Most Gracious, the Most Merciful

`Abdurahmân bin `Auf narrated that he once heard the Messenger of Allah (peace and blessings of Allah be upon him) say: Allah says, "I am ar-Rahmân (The Most Gracious). I have created the womb (Raham – family relations) and I gave it one of My names. So, whoever keeps it, surely I am related (close) to him (I will keep ties to him). And whoever severs it, surely I will stay away from him."

The word 'Ar- Rahman' has a more "stronger" and "more comprehensive" meaning than the word 'Ar-Raheem'.

Abu 'Ali Al-Farisi said: 'Ar-Rahmaan, which is exclusively for Allah, is a name that includes every kind of mercy that Allah has. Ar-Raheem is that which affects the believers, for Allah said:

And He is ever Raheem (merciful) to the believers. (33:43)

Al-'Azrami said of Ar-Rahmaan and Ar-Raheem, "He is Ar-Rahman with all creation and Ar-Rahim with the believers."

When Musaylimah the Liar called himself Rahman of Yamamah, Allah made him known by the name 'Liar' and exposed him. Therefore, whenever Musaylimah is mentioned, he is described as 'the liar'. He became an example of a liar among the inhabitants of the cities and villages and the inhabitants of the deserts, the Bedouins.

Therefore, Allah first mentioned His name - Allah - which is His alone and described this name of Ar-Rahman, which no one else is allowed to use.

As for Allah's Name Ar-Raheem, Allah has described others with this name. For example, Allah said:

Verily, there has come unto you a Messenger (Muhammad) from amongst yourselves (i.e. whom you know well). It grieves him that you should receive any injury or difficulty. He (Muhammad) is anxious over you (to be rightly guided) for the believers (he is) kind (full of pity), and Raheem (merciful)) (9:128).

Verse 2

(2) Praise be to Allah, Lord of the worlds,

These are words of praise to Allah for the perfect qualities and deeds that He performs either out of mercy or justice. All praise belongs to Him, and He is worthy of it entirely. He alone rules over all the worlds. These worlds include everything that exists except Allah Himself. He created the universe, provided its inhabitants with the means of subsistence, and blessed them with great bounties, without which they would not be able to subsist. All the blessings that bless the creatures are the gifts of the Most High Lord.

The dominion of Allah Almighty is of two kinds: universal and particular. Universal dominion is expressed in the fact that He creates creatures, sends them food and shows them the right path, thanks to which they can arrange their lives in this world. And private domination is manifested in the fact that Allah brings up His beloved servants in the spirit of piety, helps them to acquire and improve faith, protects them from everything that can lead them astray and alienate them from Him. The essence of this dominion is that Allah makes it easy for His servants the path to all good and protects them from all evil. Perhaps that is why the Prophets most often called Allah their Lord (Rabb) in their prayers. Since their aspirations were associated exclusively with the private domination of Allah Almighty.

In this revelation, the Almighty called himself the Lord of the worlds and thereby emphasized that He alone creates, governs and bestows blessings. He is rich and does not need His creations. On the contrary, all creatures need Him and are totally dependent on Him.

The Meaning of Al-Hamd

Abu Ja'far bin Jarir said, "The meaning of (Al-Hamdu Lillah) (all praise and thanks be to Allah) is: all thanks are due to Allah alone, alone, not to any of the objects worshiped instead of Him, nor to any of His creation. These thanks are due to Allah's innumerable favors and blessings, the amount of which only He knows. Allah's blessings include creating the tools that help the creation to worship Him, the physical bodies with which they are able to implement His commands, the sustenance that He gives them in this life, and the pleasant life that He has given them, without anything or anyone compelling Him to do so. Allah also warned His creation and warned them of the means and methods by which they can attain eternal abode in the abode of eternal bliss. All thanks and praise be to Allah for these services from start to finish."

Further, Ibn Jarir commented on the Ayah,

(Al-Hamdu Lillah) that it means: "A praise with which Allah praised Himself, indicating to His servants that they too should praise Him, as if Allah had said: 'Say: All thanks and praise are due to Allah." It was said that the statement,

(All praise and thanks be to Allah), involves praising Allah by mentioning His Most Beautiful Names and Most Honorable Attributes. When one proclaims, 'All thanks are due to Allah', he will thank Him for His favors and blessings."

The Difference between Praise and Thanks

Hamd is more general in that it is a praise for one's qualities, or for what he has done. Thanks (Shukr) are given for what was done, not just for characteristics.

الشكر and الحَمْدُ

are not synonyms.

Hadiths about the Virtue of Hamd of Allah

The Prophet (peace and blessings of Allah be upon him) explained that praising Allah is one form of a servant remembering Him. Allah loves praise.

1. Al-Aswad bin Sari' narrated that he once asked the Prophet, "O Messenger of Allah, would you mind if I read to you the praises that I used to pray to my Lord, the Most Holy and Most High?" The Messenger of Allah replied, "Remember, indeed your Lord Azza wa Jalla loves praise (likes Al-Hamd)."

2. Anas bin Malik narrated that Rasulullah (peace and blessings of Allah be upon him) said, "Not once does Allah give favors to a servant, then the

servant says, "Praise be to Allah", but what Allah gives (in the form of inspiration to say alhamdulillah) is more important than just what he receives."

Imam al-Qurthubi interprets this hadith: When a servant gets favors and then speaks, the inspiration that Allah gives him to utter sentences (which praise Allah) is truly more enjoyable than all worldly pleasures. Therefore, the reward of praising Allah will last forever even though the world has perished. Therefore, the pronunciation of Al-Hamdulillah (the praising of Allah) is more important than the pleasure itself.

Sayings of the Salaf about Al-Hamd

Hafs mentioned that 'Umar said to 'Ali (Allah be pleased with them): "We know La ilaha illallah, Subhan Allah and Allahu Akbar. What about Al-Hamdu Lillah?" 'Ali said: "A statement that Allah liked for Himself, was pleased with for Himself, and He likes it to be repeated."

Ibn 'Abbas (Allah be pleased with him) said: "Al-Hamdu Lillah is the declaration of appreciation. When the servant says Al-Hamdu Lillah, Allah says: 'My servant has praised Me.'

The letters Alif and Laam before the word Hamd serve to encompass all kinds of thanks and appreciation for Allah, the Most High.

Meaning of Rabbil 'Alamin

The word means "Lord of the Worlds".

The word means the Owner who has the right to act, which according to the language shows the meaning of the master and the entity who is free to do things for improvement. Each of these meanings is in accordance with the rights of Allah.

Allah is the Almighty God. God who works for His servants for good and guarantees them.

The word that is expressed singly (Ar-Rabb) is only meant for Allah.

The meaning of Al-'Alamin

Al-'Alamin is the plural of 'Alam, which includes everything that exists except Allah. The word 'Alam is itself a plural word that has no singular form. 'Alamin are various creations found in heaven and on earth, on land and in water. Each generation of creation is called an 'Alam. Al-Farra' and Abu 'Ubayd said: "'Alam includes everything that has a mind, the jinn, mankind, the angels and devils, but not the animals." Also Zayd bin Aslam and Abu Muhaysin said: 'Alam includes all that Allah has created with a soul.'

Qatadah said about 'Lord of Alamin': "Every form of creation is an 'Alam." Az-Zajjaj also said, "Alam includes everything that Allah created, in this life and in the Hereafter." Al-Qurtubi commented: "This is the correct meaning that 'Alam includes everything that Allah created in both worlds. Similarly, Allah said:

Fir'awn (Pharaoh) said: "And what is the Lord of the 'Alamin (worlds)?" Musa (Moses) said: "The Lord of the heavens and the earth, and all that is between them, (that is your God) if you seek to be convinced with certainty") (26:23-24).

Alam is derived from 'Alamah, that is because it is a sign that testifies to the existence of its Creator and to His Oneness."

Ibnul Mu'taz wrote about this:

How strange why disobedience to God
Or why someone does not believe
His existence
In fact, in everything that exists there is a sign
that shows that He is the One.

Verse 3

(3) The Most Gracious, The Most Merciful.

The meanings of these words has been adequately discussed in the discussion of basmalah.

Imam al-Qurtubi said that the wisdom in mentioning the words (Ar-Rahmaan and Ar-Raheem) and after hamdalah is to combine targhib (motivate) and tarhib (scare). This is often found in the Qur'an, for example:

Inform My servants that indeed I am the Most Forgiving, Most Merciful, and that My punishment is indeed a very painful punishment. (al-Hijr [15]:49-50)

Verily, your Lord is swift in punishment and verily He is Most Forgiving, Most Merciful. (al-An'am [6]: 165)

The phrase "Rabbul Aalamin" is Tarhib (to scare), and the phrase "Most Gracious, Most Merciful" is Targhib (to motivate, to have hope). This is so that a believer combines the two in him.

Abu Hurairah (Allah be pleased with him) narrated that the Messenger of Allah (peace and blessings of Allah be upon him) said,

If the believers knew what kind of torment is with Allah, surely no one would covet His paradise. If the disbeliever knew what kind of mercy is with Allah, surely no one would despair of His mercy.

Verse 4

(4) Lord of the Day of Retribution!

The Ruler is called the One who has the kingdom and power and, because of this, is free to command and forbid, reward and punish, and have full authority to dispose of His subordinates. Who owns the true power, it will become clear on the Day of Retribution. This is one of the descriptions of the Day of Resurrection, when people will receive retribution for their good and bad deeds. It is on that day that God's creatures will clearly see the perfection of Allah's power, the perfection of His justice and wisdom. They will lose everything they had before. Kings and subjects, slaves and freemen - all will be equal before the Lord, obedient to His majesty and humble before His might. They will await His judgment, yearn for His reward, and fear His retribution. That is why the Lord called himself the Ruler of the Day of Retribution, although His power extends to all time.

Ownership belongs only to Allah, the Ruler of that Day.

Allah said,

Verily, We inherit the earth and all those who are on it. And only to Us they are returned. (Maryam [19]: 40)

Say, "I take refuge in God (Who Preserves and Rules) mankind. The King of mankind." (an-Nas [114]: 1-2)

The meaning of this verse is, "The kingdom, power, commands, and prohibitions on the Day of Judgment belong only to Allah. No one can match Him.".

On the day they came out (from the graves), nothing was hidden before Allah. To whom does the kingdom today belong? It only belongs to Allah, the One and Only, the All-Conqueror. (al-Mu'min [40]: 16)

Allah mentioned His sovereignty on the Day of Judgement, but this does not negate His sovereignty over all other things. For Allah mentioned that He is the Lord of existence, including this worldly life and the Hereafter. Allah only mentioned the Day of Judgment here because on that day no one but Him will be able to claim ownership of anything. On that day no one will speak without His permission.

Allah said,

On the Day when Ar-Ruh (Jibril (Gabriel) or another angel) and the angels will stand forth in rows, they will not speak except him whom the Most Merciful (Allah) allows, and he will say what is right. (78:38)

And all voices will be humble for the Most Merciful (Allah), and you will hear nothing but the quiet voice of their footsteps. (20:108)

Ad-Dahhak said that Ibn 'Abbas commented: "Allah says, 'On that Day, no one will own what he had owned previously in this world.'"

The meaning of the name Yaum Ad-Din

Ibn 'Abbas said: "Yaum ad-Din is the Day of Retribution for the creatures, that is, the Day of Judgment. On that day, Allah will reckon the creatures for their deeds, evil for evil, good for good, except for those whom He forgives."

In addition, several other Companions, the Tabieen and learned Salaf, said the same thing, for this meaning is obvious and clear from the verse.

Allah is Al-Malik (King or Owner)

Allah is the True Owner (Malik) (of everything and everyone). Allah said:

He is Allah, besides Whom La ilaha illa Huva, King, Holy, Free from all shortcomings) (59:23).

Also, in the Two Saheehs, Abu Hurayrah reports that the Prophet (peace and blessings of Allah be upon him) said:

The most despicable name to Allah is a man who calls himself the King of Kings, while there are no masters but Allah.

The Prophet (peace and blessings of Allah be upon him) said:

"On the Day of Judgment) Allah will seize the earth and fold up the heavens with His Right Hand and proclaim: "I am the King! Where are the kings of the earth? Where are the tyrants? Where are the arrogant?'"

The meaning of the name Ad-Din

Ad-din means retribution, the reward or punishment.

Likewise, Allah said:

On that day, Allah will reward them (dinahum) recompense (for their deeds) in full) (24:25), and,

Shall we (rise) in order to receive reward or punishment (according to our deeds)?) (37:53)

A hadith says,

اَلْكَيِّسُ مَنْ دَانَ نَفْسَهُ وَعَمِلَ لِمَا بَعْدَ الْمَوتِ

(A wise man is one who reckons himself and works for (his life) after death.) That is, he considers himself responsible. Also 'Umar said: "Take responsibility before you are called to account, weigh yourself before you are weighed, and be ready for the biggest gathering before the One Whose knowledge embraces your deeds."

(5) You alone we worship and You alone we pray for help.

This means: we worship only You alone and only You pray for help. In accordance with the grammar of the Arabic language, if the pronoun comes before the verb, then the action is performed only in relation to the person mentioned and no one else. Therefore, the revelation we are discussing has the following meaning: we worship You and do not worship anyone else, and we cry for help to You and do not cry for help to anyone else.

Worship is mentioned before the plea for help, and such a turn is an example of including the particular in the general, because when listing the general, it is customary to mention the general before the particular. Along with this, such a sequence of words indicates that the right of Allah Almighty is higher than the right of His slaves.

Worship is a concept that encompasses all words and deeds performed by both the soul and the body, which Allah loves and approves. A prayer for help is an appeal to Allah Almighty with a request to bestow good and protect from evil, imbued with the belief that this will certainly come true.

It is worship and prayer for help that are the right way to gain eternal happiness and get rid of all evil. Apart from this, there is no other way to salvation. That is why it is very important to know that worship acquires its true meaning only when it is done for the sake of Allah in full accordance with the instructions of His Messenger, peace and blessings of Allah be upon him. Without the fulfillment of these two conditions, no worship is possible.

Despite the fact that the prayer for help is one of the forms of worship, Almighty Allah mentioned it separately, because when performing any worship, the servant of Allah needs the help of his Lord. Without His help, a person will never be able to properly fulfill God's commands and avoid sins.

(6) Guide us to the straight path,

This means: show us a straight path, guide us to it and help us follow it. This clear path leads to Allah and ends in Paradise, and only those who know the truth and are guided by it in their deeds can pass along it.

It also means: lead us to the straight path and guide us along it. The first involves the conversion to Islam and the renunciation of all other faiths, and the second - the study of the laws of religion and their implementation in practice. This prayer is one of the most useful, deep and comprehensive prayers in Islam. Allah obligated people to call on Him with these words in every rak'ah of prayer, because every person needs God's help.

صِرَٰطَ ٱلَّذِينَ أَنْعَمْتَ عَلَيْهِمْ غَيْرِ ٱلْمَغْضُوبِ عَلَيْهِمْ وَلَا ٱلضَّآلِّينَ ۝

(7) the way of those whom You have favored, not those on whom anger fell, and not those who went astray.

The straight path is the path of the prophets, the true believers, the fallen martyrs and the righteous, whom Almighty Allah has blessed. This is not the way of those who fell under His wrath because they saw the truth but turned away from it. It was this fate that befell the Jews and their ilk. And this is not the way of those who have gone astray, who have turned away from the truth because of their ignorance and misguidance, like Christians and the like.

Despite its conciseness, this surah contains something that is not found in any other Qur'anic surah. It reflects the three components of monotheism (Tawheed). Belief in the dominance of Allah alone is formulated in the words "To the Lord of the worlds." The belief that only Allah is worthy of worship is expressed in the very name "Allah" and in the words "You alone we worship and You alone we pray for help." And the belief that only Allah has beautiful names and perfect qualities (attributes) stems from the words "praise be to Allah," as mentioned earlier. This component of monotheism implies belief in all the names and qualities of the Almighty Allah, by which He himself described Himself and by which the Prophet Muhammad described Him. At the same time, the divine qualities cannot be deprived of their true meaning and likened to the qualities of creations.

This surah also contains proof of the truth of the prophetic mission of Muhammad, which is expressed in the words "Guide us to the straight path." Indeed, this would not have been possible if there had not been a prophetic message.

The words "To the Lord of the Day of Retribution" contain an indication that people will certainly receive retribution for their deeds. This retribution will be just, because the word *din* ('retribution') implies just retribution.

This surah also exposes the fallacy of the views of the Qadarites and Jabris, since it states that everything that exists happens according to the predestination of Allah, despite the fact that people have the right to choose. Moreover, it refutes the views of all adherents of heretical and erring movements, for the words "lead us to the straight path" encourage Muslims to know the truth and be guided by it in their deeds. As for the adherents of heresy (people of innovation – Bid'aah), religious innovations and misguidance, each of them will certainly turn away from direct guidance.

Along with this, this surah contains a call for sincere service to Allah Almighty and seeking help only from Him. This is the meaning of the words "You alone we worship and You alone we pray for help." Praise be to Allah, the Lord of the worlds!

Summary of Al-Fatiha

The honorable Surah Al-Fatiha contains seven verses, including the praise and gratitude of Allah, the glorification of Him and the praise of Him by mentioning His Most Beautiful Names and the highest Attributes. It also mentions the Hereafter, which is the Day of Resurrection, and directs the servants of Allah to ask Him by calling out to Him alone and declaring that all power and strength comes from Him alone. It also calls for the sincerity of worshiping only Allah, highlighting Him in His divinity, believing in His perfection, being free from the need for any partners, having no rivals and equals. Al-Fatihah tells the believers to call on Allah to guide them to the straight path which is the true religion and help them stay on that path in this life and to pass the real Sirat (the bridge over hell that everyone must pass above) on the Judgment day. On that day, believers will be directed to the gardens of comfort in the company of the prophets, the truthful, the martyrs and the righteous. Al-Fatiha also encourages doing good deeds so that the believers will be in the company of those who do good on the Day of Resurrection. The surah also warns against following the paths of error, so that on the Day of Resurrection you will not be with those who indulge in sin, including those who deserve wrath and those who have been led astray.

Praise be to Allah, the Lord of the worlds!

www.ingramcontent.com/pod-product-compliance
Lightning Source LLC
Chambersburg PA
CBHW031413160726
47993CB00003B/1212